ADÉLIE & THE BEAR

Adélie and the Bear LLC

Text and illustrations copyright © 2024 by Megan Levaque.
All rights reserved. No reproduction of the work in part or in whole without consent.

This book was typeset in Baskerville.
The illustrations were done in watercolor, pen and ink and colored pencil.
ISBN 979-8-9852094-3-3

And because everyone loved it in Dance to the Moon,
you can find a butterfly and a ladybug on almost every spread again!

For Olivia, Milo & Charles, always.

When Dreams Collide

The sequel to *Dance to the Moon*

MEGAN LEVAQUE

What do you do after your dream comes true?
Especially when that dream was dancing to the moon!
Olivia and Milo could still feel the magic of their journey waltzing in their toes
and as they looked at the moon from their new favorite spot, another idea arose.

"If we can dance to the moon," Olivia started,
"can you imagine what else we can do?
We can build the highest tower! We can solve the most unsolved clue!
We can dive to the bottom of the ocean
and explore the seven seas!
Oh, Milo! Get the pen and paper!
Can you picture all the possibilities!?"

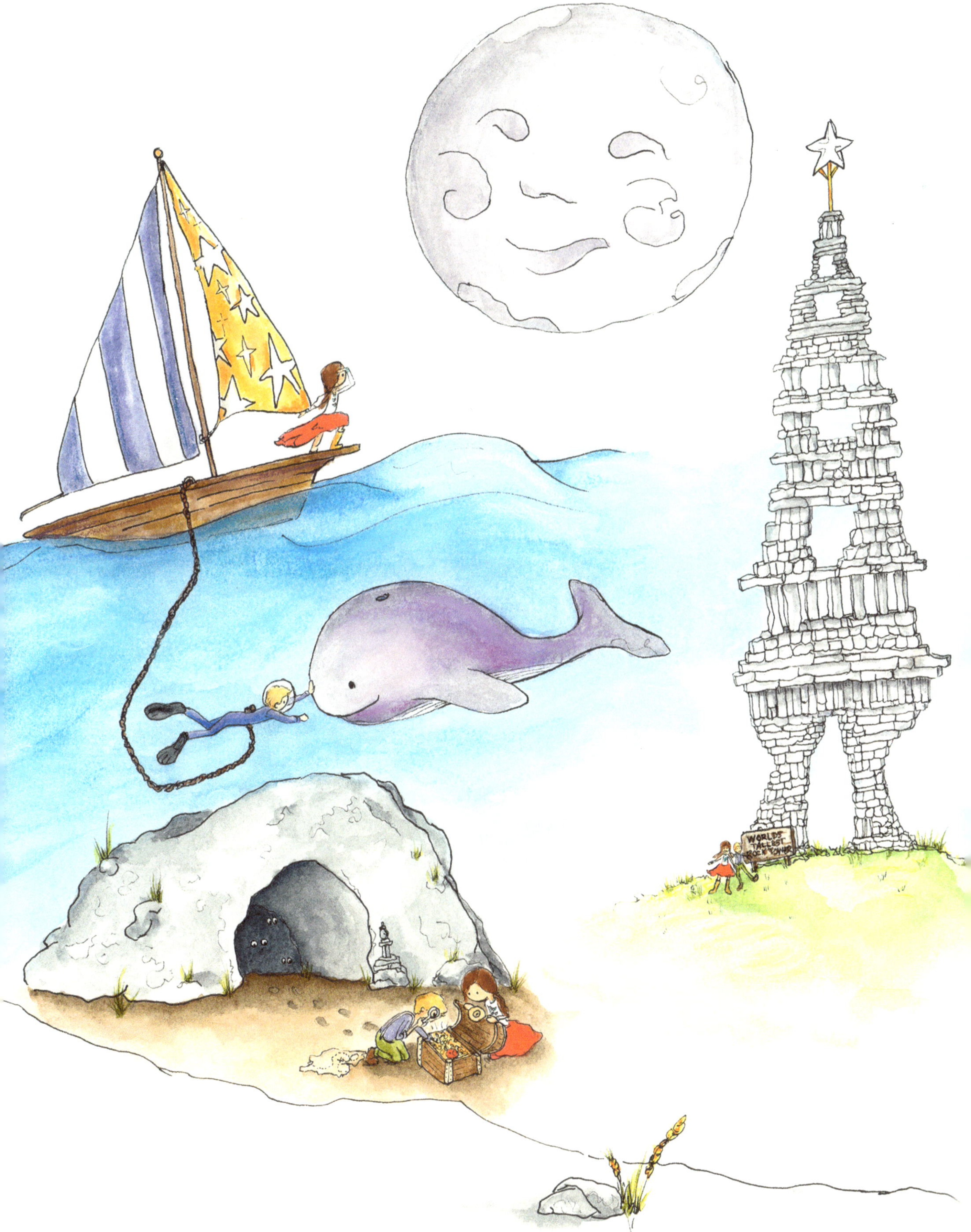
WORLDS TALLEST ROCK TOWER

Milo stood there still staring at the moon.
He did see all the possibilities and knew exactly what to do.

"We climbed and we danced to the moon," Milo began,
"and I'll forever feel the power of believing and that **magic** in my bones.
Now let's help others **chase their dreams**
when all they see are the unknowns!"

It was as if a **firework burst** in their hearts. There was no time to lose.
A dream was out there to be chased, they just did not know whose.

What a daunting task! It certainly would not be short and sweet.
But if you know these two, they won't stop until their mission is complete!

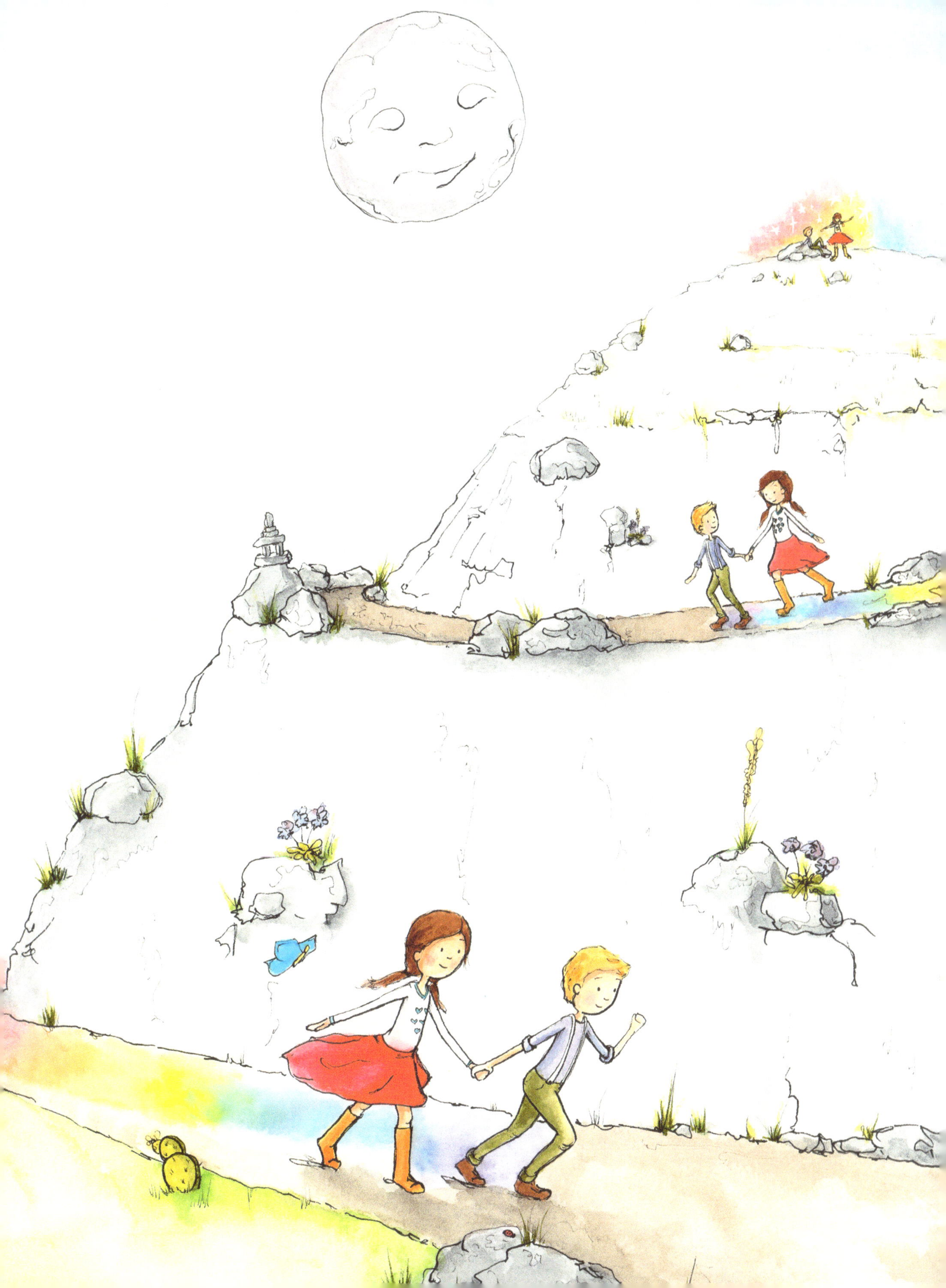

Down the mountain they went
and it didn't take long til they ran into Bear.
He was surprised and quite joyous to hear
of their journey to the moon that they did share.

"That's magnificent! It's profound!" He said.
"I am oh so proud of you two!
It's really quite inspiring.
I didn't believe dreams like that could come true!
I also have a wild dream,
but it has always felt too lofty for me.
It's impossible. Awfully silly.
And if I'm honest, it's also quite scary."

"Well, you know, Bear," said Milo,

"When you put a dream out into the world,

it becomes alive.

And we're here to help you chase that dream!

We won't leave your side."

"And remember," Olivia chimed in,

"nothing is impossible. Nothing is too silly either.

Tell us what that dream is

and we'll help make you a believer!"

Bear sat up tall, took a deep breath
and began to speak with a heart full of hope.
"Well, here it is then. I want to walk between two mountains -
but up high on a tightrope!"

"That does sound scary," Milo started,
"and a little wild, that is true.
But our dream is to help you chase your dream
and that's exactly what we'll do."

When a dream unfolds it is thrilling
and that thrill makes you reach higher.
And when you work together,
well, that dream spreads like wildfire.

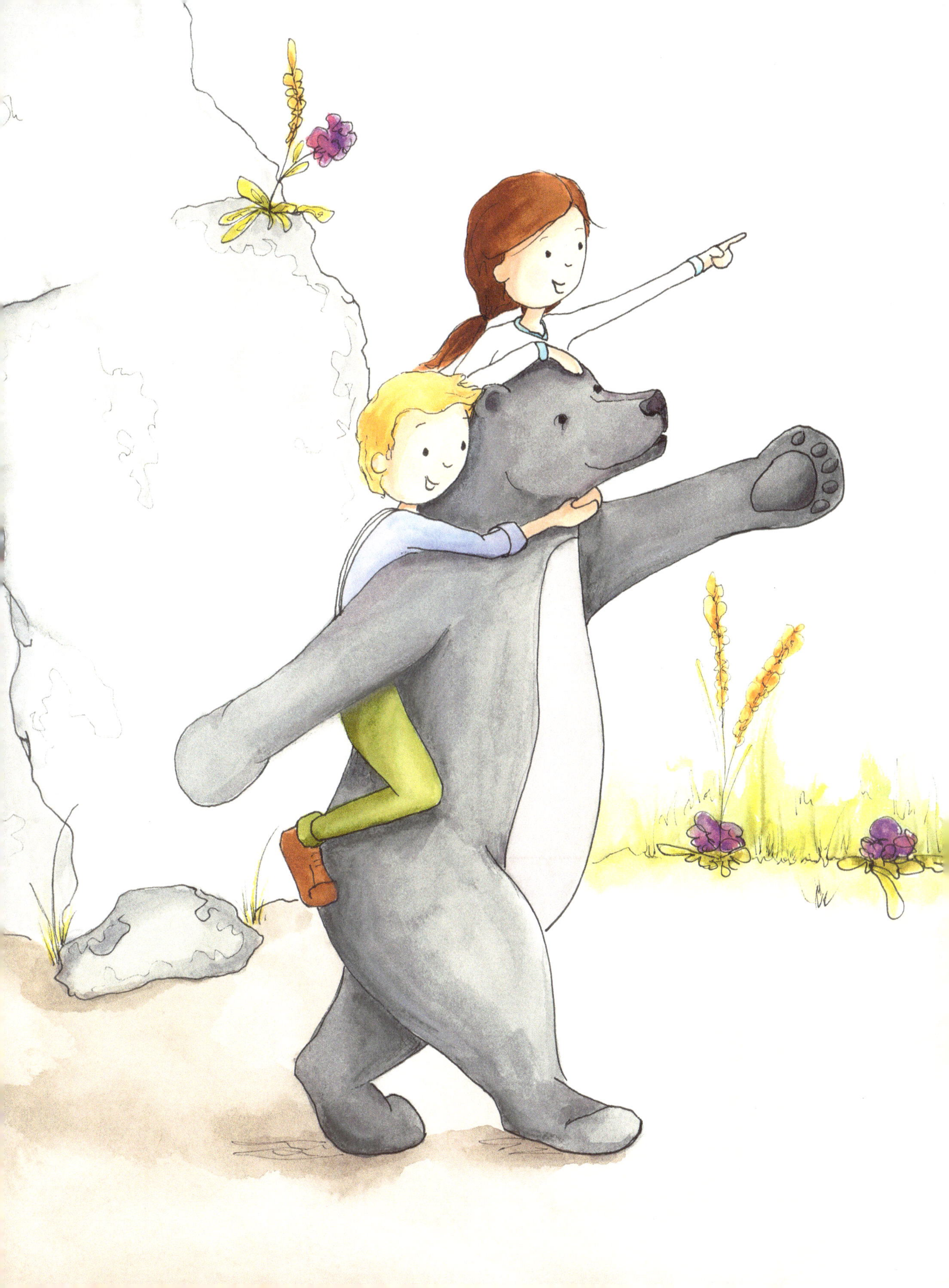

Squirrel and Mr. Owl soon arrived
to also hear of the successful moon mission.
And Bear told them about his tightrope dream.
Both were eager to listen.

Mr. Owl, clearly ecstatic, was joyous at the news!
But Squirrel - not so much.
She put her paws on her hips and shook her head.
She'd had quite enough.

"First it was dancing to the moon," Squirrel started, "now walking on a tightrope. I say mission abort! These dreams are rubbish! Dangerous! Absurd! You certainly do not have my support."

Squirrel hurried off in a fury and ran out of sight.

Olivia, Milo and Mr. Owl still believed in Bear. This was not up for debate. The team got right to work as there was absolutely no time to waste.

Together the friends practiced balancing on branches as well as fallen trees.
Bear started to feel **confident**. He could do it all with ease.

There was one thing he failed to mention:
Bear was scared of heights.
Balancing on branches was pretty easy,
but the thought of that tightrope gave him the frights.

Olivia and Milo gave him a hug
and then Milo stood upon Bear's knee.
He took Bear's face into his hands
and made a heartfelt plea.

"You may be scared.
That feeling is real and true.
But you are also capable!
You are enough!
You need to believe in you!"

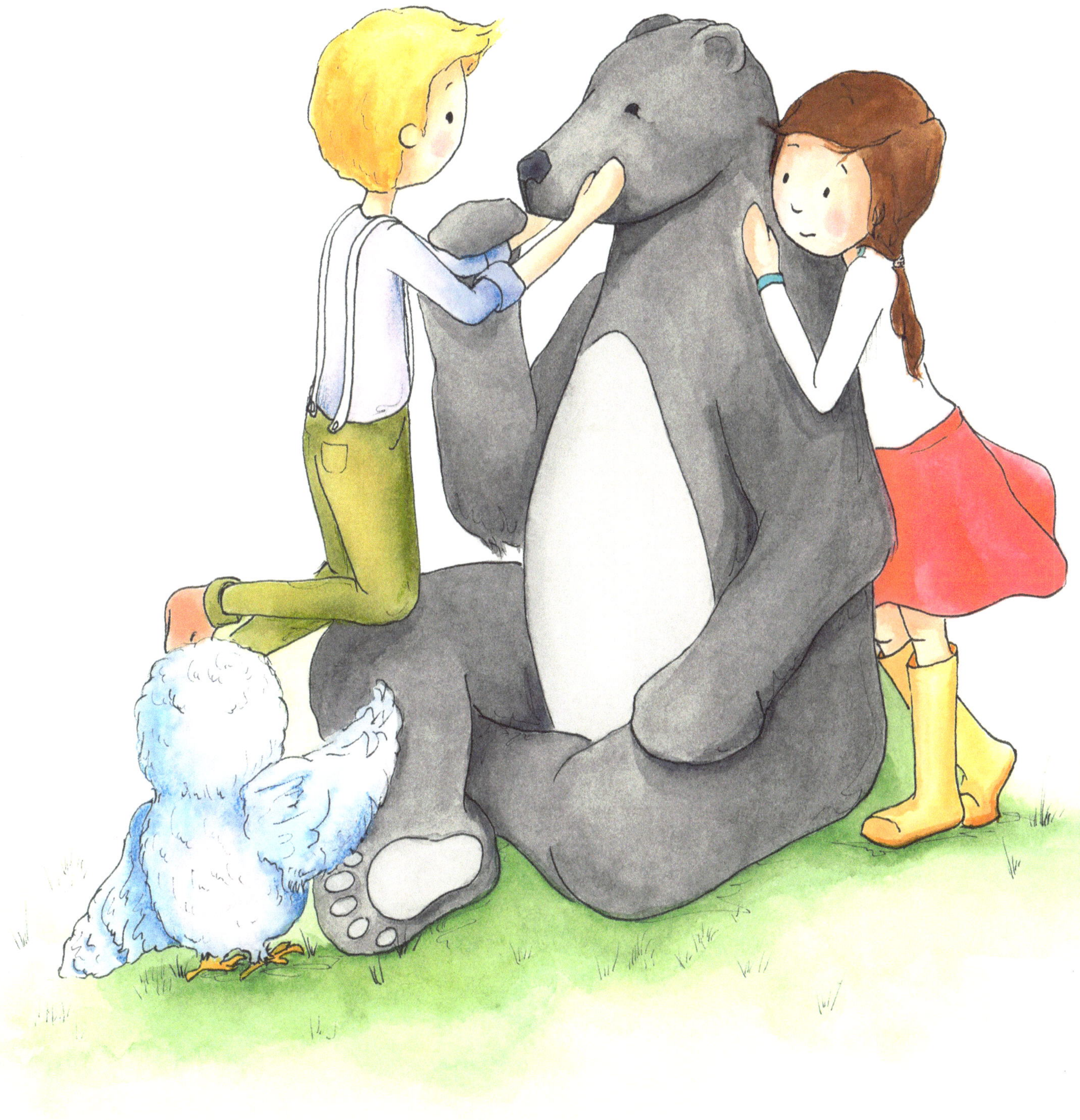

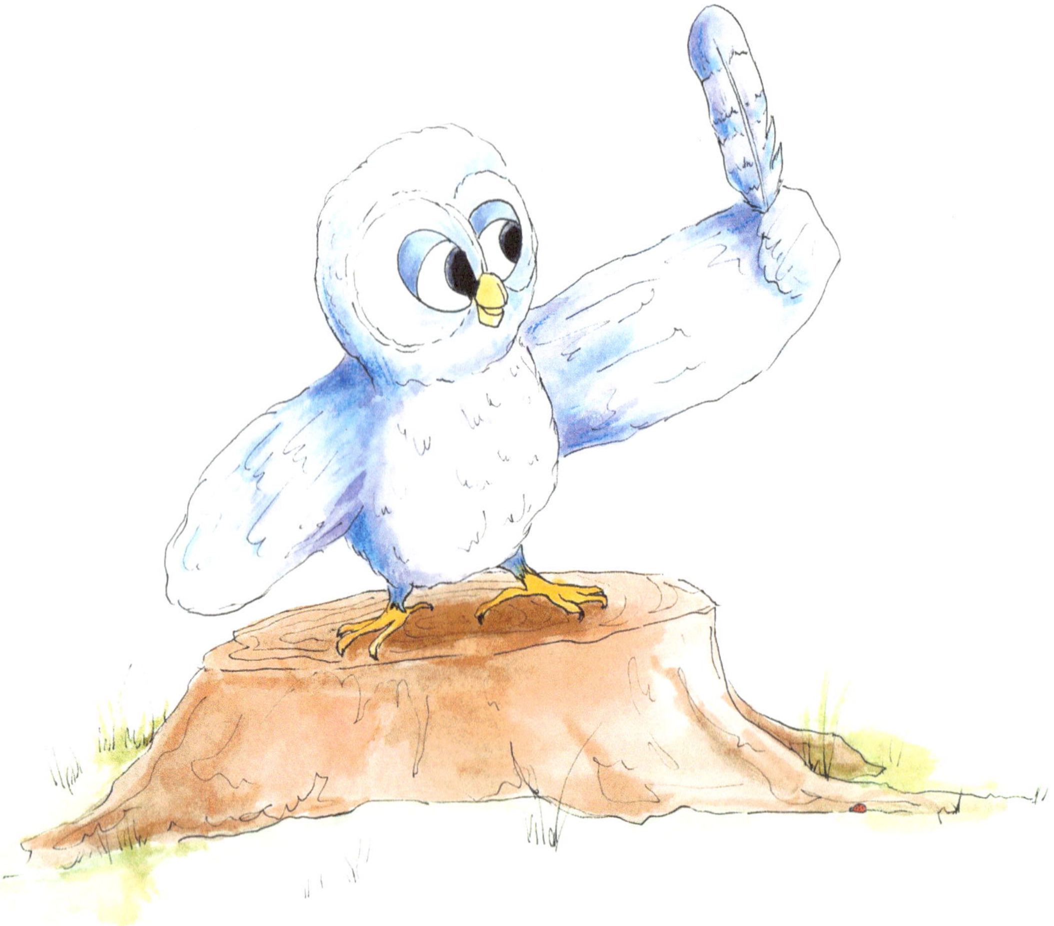

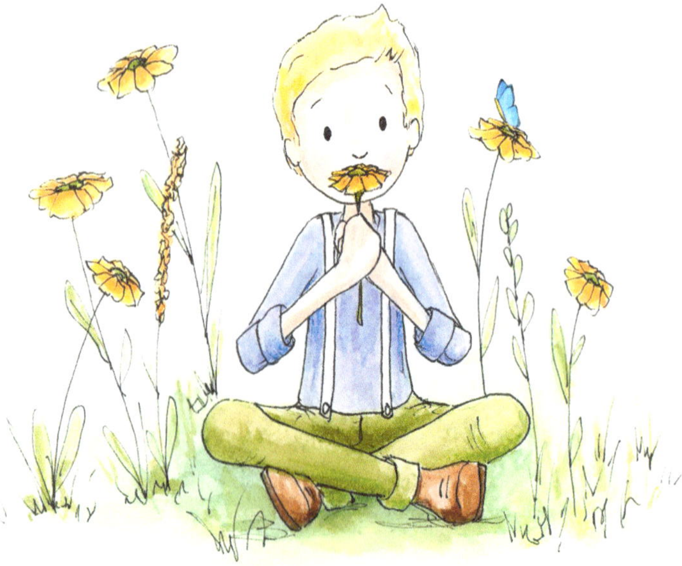

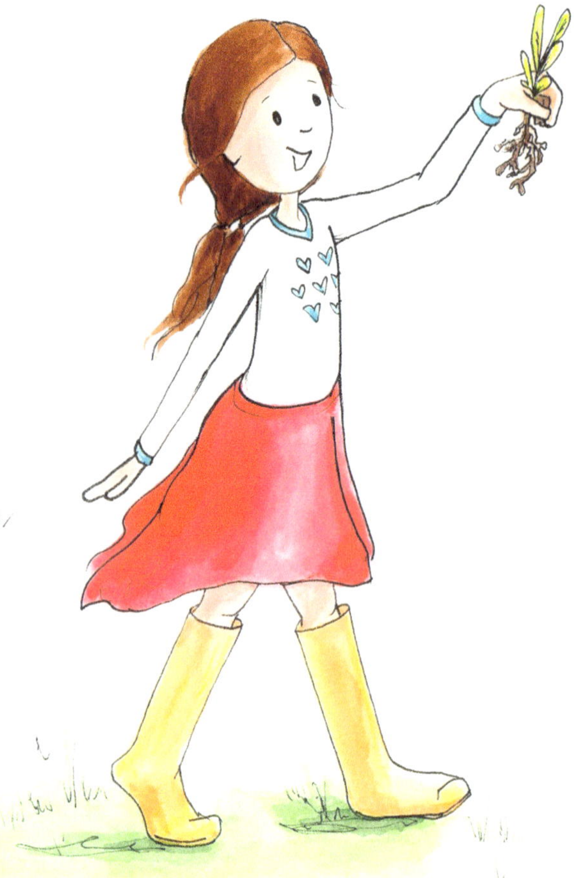

"It's okay to be scared," Olivia stepped in,

"and if you change your mind, that's also okay.

Either decision you go with, know that you're still really quite brave.

But I have an idea so you don't feel alone while you're up high above."

So together they made Bear a Crown of Courage to help him feel their love.

"A leaf for lightness!" Mr. Owl sang.

"A flower for brightness!" Milo added.

"A root to help you feel strong!" Olivia began,

"And don't forget your smile for balance

when the wind nudges you along!"

Bear held that crown in his hands
and placed it upon his head.
He took a deep breath and spoke
these words to get rid of his dread.
"I may be scared
and that's a fine feeling to be.
But I am also capable!
I am enough!
I believe in me!"

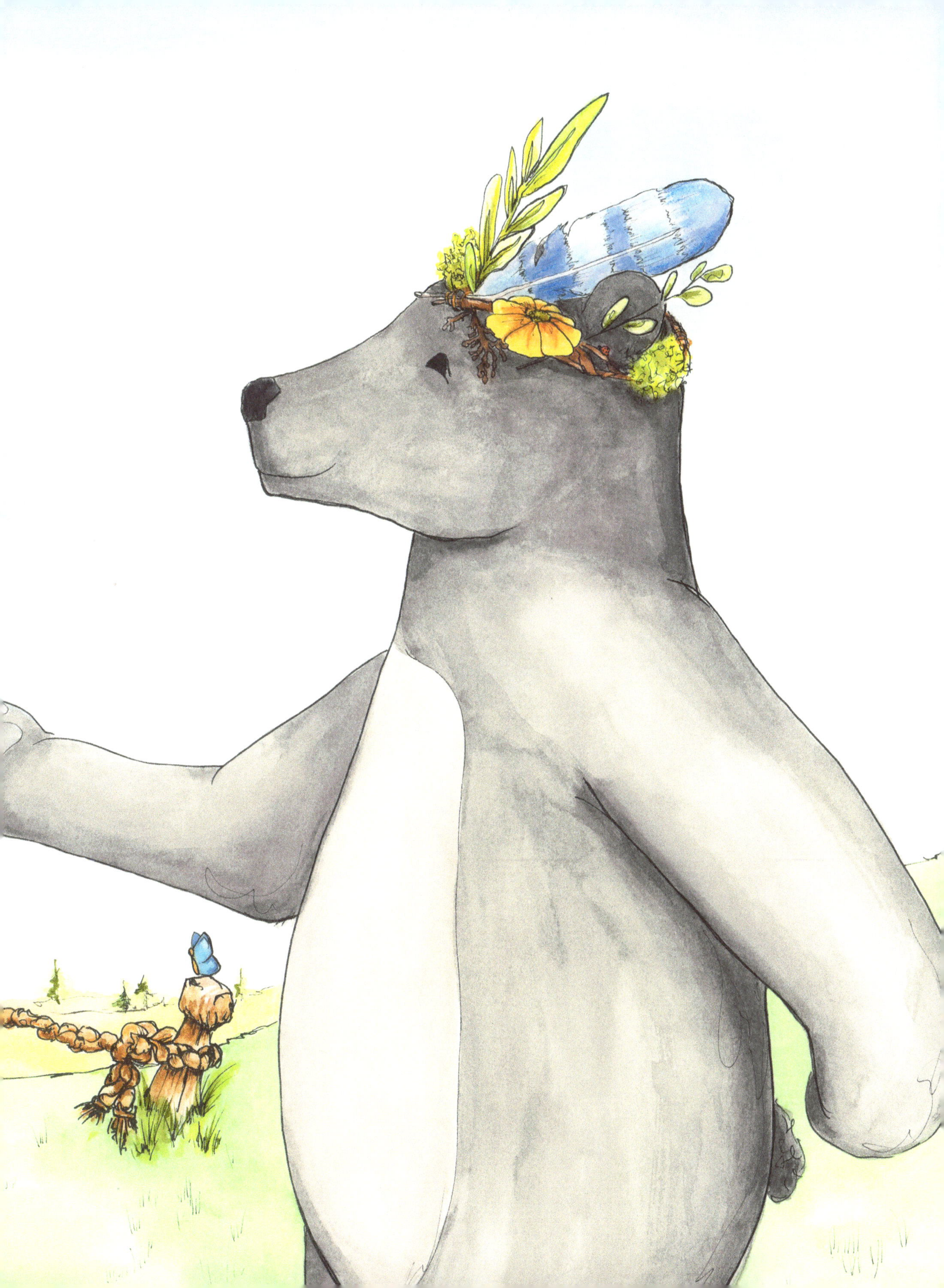

With his new confidence
Bear took his first step,
and another after that.
Before he knew it,
Bear was halfway there!
His Crown of Courage kept him on track.
He was light. He was free.
He could feel that courage from his crown.
But then Bear lost his balance
when he happened to look down.

He wobbled to the left.

And then way more to the right.

Bear lost his courage.

He was totally terrified.

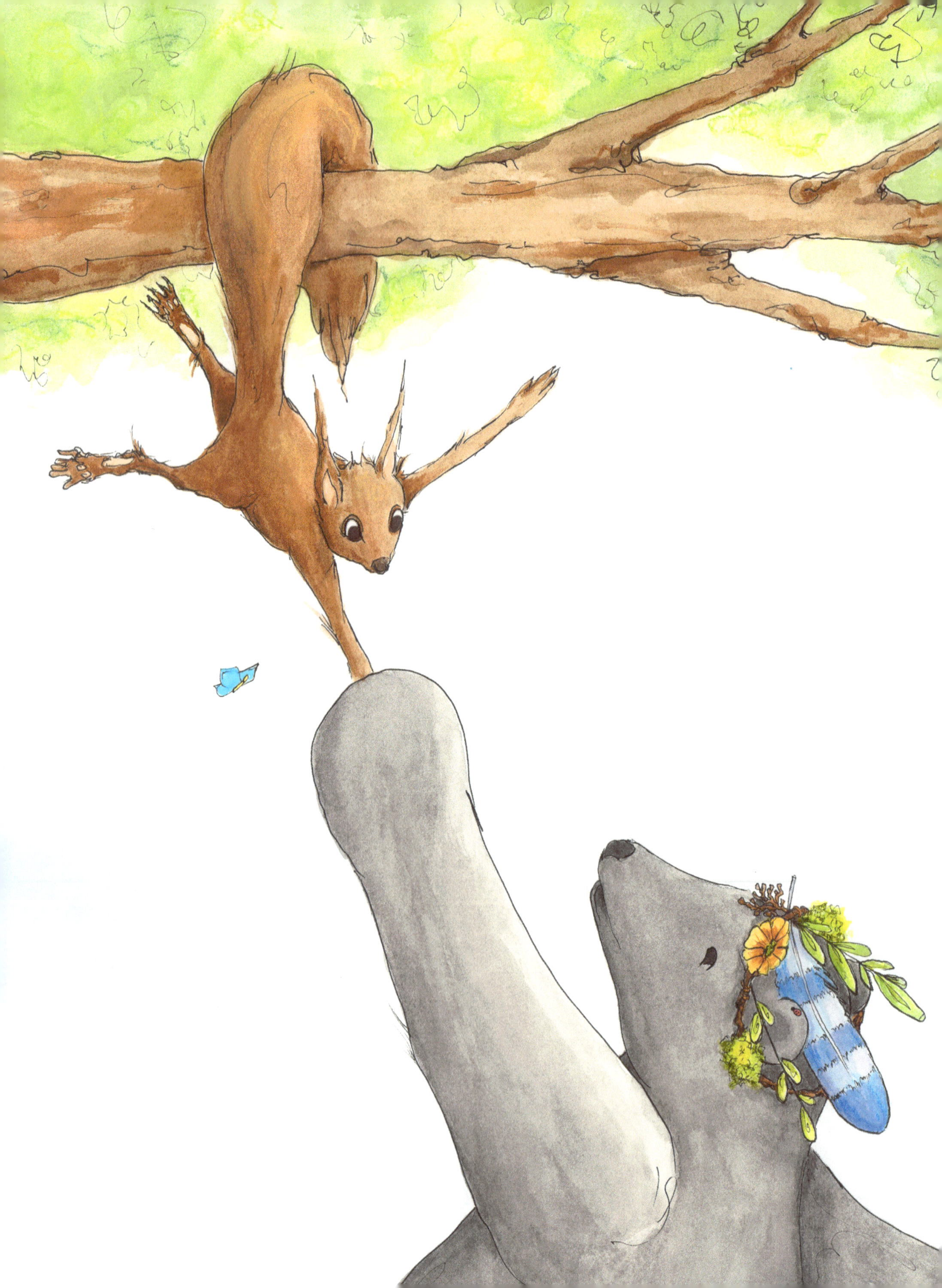

And then it happened. He completely lost balance.
But as he fell he looked up in awe.
Because at the very last second Bear was caught
By the tiniest little paw.

He was astonished and the most grateful bear
in the whole entire world.
For the friend that saved him from falling
was none other than Squirrel.

"Don't look down," she said,
"You got this. Just keep your eyes on me."
They held tightly onto each other and with her help,
Bear was able to succeed.

Stepping off the tightrope, Bear set Squirrel upon his palm as he leaned against the tree.

"You left quite upset earlier," Bear said. "What made you come back for me?"

"When I left you all back there," she began, "I met a miraculous creature. They taught me about love and dreams and also made me a believer."

"I'm sorry I doubted you, Bear.
Your dream sounded scary and I was quite afraid."
Then she placed a beautiful star in his crown and smiled.
"But you, my friend, are really, truly brave."

Olivia, Milo and Mr. Owl bounded up the ridge
with praise so cheerful and sweet.
Bear looked all around him - he felt enormously proud
now that his mission was complete!

But he was more joyous about the help from his friends,
for their love glowed so bright.
And that magic swirled around them.
It was the most magnificent sight!

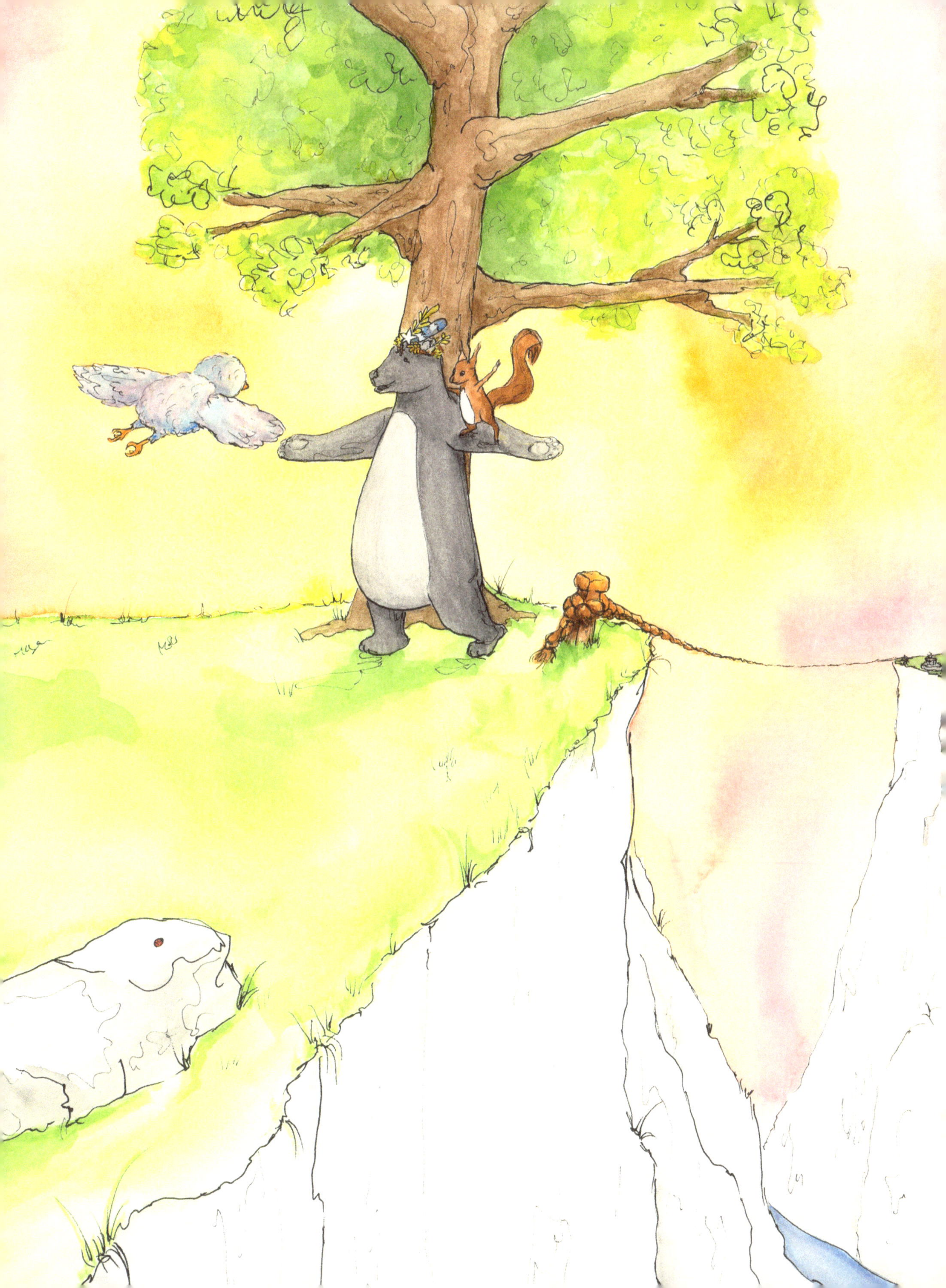

This is the magic that happens when our dreams collide
and the twists and turns of imagination begin to take flight.
Our ideas and wonders catapult from our mind,
and the colors are radiant, magnificent, divine.

So if you have the magic,

spread it around as much as you can.

Because while a smile can change the world,

so can lending a hand.

The end

Make your own
Crown of Courage

Now is the time to go **explore!** Take a walk in your backyard and around your neighborhood. What can you find in nature to make your own Crown of Courage? We all need a little help sometimes when it comes to being brave. Who will you give it to? Do you know someone that might need it?

Or could it be for you?

A leaf for lightness!
A flower for brightness!
A root to help you feel strong!
And don't forget
your smile
for balance
when the wind
nudges you along!

Megan Levaque

After writing and illustrating Dance to the Moon, Megan knew these characters had one more adventure up their sleeve. And what better way to get the group together than to help one another chase a dream! Always inspired by her own Olivia and Milo, Megan enjoys exploring with her family in their town of Fort Collins, Colorado and welcomes any and all adventures on the horizon.

Milton Keynes UK
Ingram Content Group UK Ltd.
UKHW051415240424
441669UK00004B/23